THE SEARCH

THE SEARCH

J. DAVID SOLOMON

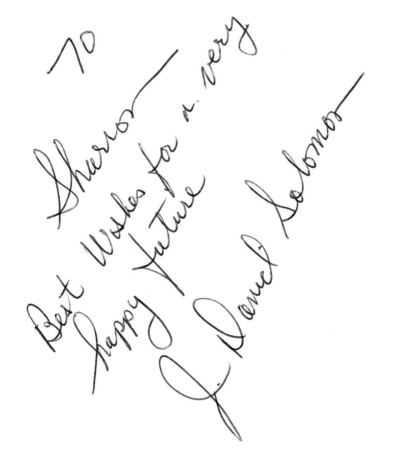

To Sharron

Best Wishes for a very happy future

J. David Solomon

ISBN 0-9662119-0-1
Library of Congress Catalog No. 97-077799

WORDSMITH–SUTHERLAND, INC.
Detroit, Michigan
313/864-8292
e-mail: wspublish@aol.com

In Memory of
Daniel and Ella Hughes

THANKS TO:

My Creator, My Savior, My Comfort

My Mother for her Unconditional Love, Faith and Support

My Wife for her undying love and patience

Jena East for planting the seed.
And *Common Ground News*, Harrisburg Pennsylvania
For publishing my work.

Ms Ann Jackson, University of the District of Columbia

Special thanks to Dr. Alan Lefcowitz, and
The Writers Center in Bethesda, Md for their pivotal support

Barbara Shaw: Book design and page layouts
Herman Busey: Trademark design and artwork

TABLE OF CONTENTS

INSPIRATION

From the cradle
And even before,
The search begins.
Things to touch,
Things to taste,
To feel in our mouths
To test and sample,
To hold and Possess.
And so, on through life

We grow more,
We know more,
We show more
We gain and we obtain
But we don't know what for
And though the senses find satisfaction
And life is filled with every attraction
We still can't find the open door.

Every day we rise
Looking again for that perfect ending
That single word of inspiration
That one true love that never came
That place of rest where Peace flows
Like a gentle river.

And, as we go through our day
The soul stands alert and on guard
That at any instant it should appear
The heart may rejoice

And Peace might rush over us
Like the incoming tide
And Journey will have United with Destiny.

But until then, the Search, goes on.

There must be a wonderful morning somewhere
A dawn lit by justice and judgment is fair
A place where a helping hand is always held out
An ear that will listen stands poised and devout

A place you can go when your heart needs attending
A place where a spirit gets healing and mending
A place where love's fire burns bright day and night
And in from the cold you may warm by its light

There must be a wonderful evening somewhere
Where the sun finally sets on pain and despair
Where the coming of night is not filled with grief
And comforting sleep brings you joyful relief

A place where the sunset is apt to reflect
A day without malice, without disrespect
A place where the only tears shed, are for joy
And a heart is not battered and bounced like a toy

There must be a wonderful day somewhere
In a place filled with love and a great need to care
A place where the burdens of conflict are lifted
Where love is a skill and all lovers are gifted

Where daily are spoken the words that support
And every mistake is not met with retort
A place where the land has not soaked up the blood
Where honor and truth are not cast in the mud

A Place where the children are not left alone
Where Sisters and Brothers may come to atone
Where homeless and helpless don't cower in fright
Where the hearts and the minds of the world can unite

So you set on a journey to seek out this land
With compass and map and a vision so grand
To find peace and comfort in a world thats so new
Where waters are crystal and skies are so blue

With showers that cleanse and winds that refresh
Where the spirit is fed and not just the flesh
But search as you may, what you'll find to be true
That it can not be found, 'til it's found within you

LOVE

Did you ever wonder
How the sun moves through the skies
Or how the flowers seek the rays
Of warmth at mornings rise

Did you ever stop to think about
Just how the Lilies grow
Or how the roses come to bloom
In colors of the bow

Did you ever stop to ponder
As the world is turning 'round
Just how my love is sown for you
In deep and fertile ground

And if you sit and watch it
You will never see it move
But all the while its blossoming
Its beauty just to prove

I could only see you from a distance
I could only see you from afar
I could never see an imperfection
I could only see you as a star

I could only see your beauty shining
I could only see your lighted face
I could only see your graceful movements
And the elegance you embrace

But I never had a chance to touch you
Or to see the sunlight in your eye
But I saw the glory He put in you
That Illuminates the evening sky

Now I know that none of us are perfect
We all have some iniquity
But the love and beauty deep within you
Is all I really longed to see

I awoke this morning
I first heard the sound
Of a singing bird, so soft, so alive
It was your voice

I opened my eyes this morning
I saw radiant light beaming
Soft and penetrating through
The window of my soul
It was your face

As I drew my first deep breath this morning
I smelled the freshness of the flowers
That seduces the honey bee
And causes it to come near
It was your skin

How awesome it is to know that
God has adorned you with
The beauty of His creations
And made you a Queen

I just can't quite make a connection
It's nowhere in my recollection
But there's something about the awesome powers
Of making love and April showers

I just don't know what makes it better
Who could explain it to the letter
Just what the falling rain can do
As love rains down on me and you

The drenching sounds pour in my ears
And make my eyes well up with tears
And lights my fire not to mention
My every nerve is at attention

Oh how the pitter patter sound
Goes through my soul, I spin around
I fall into your warm embrace
With kisses wet upon your face

Now, here my love we break the glasses
And fall into the warm wet grasses
And as the rain falls on our skin
Explodes the passion, deep within

Our hearts take flight in ecstasy
And floods of joy wash you and me
Oh, wonderful this celebration
So far beyond our expectation

So precious is this love so true
Sensations shared by me and you
Are magnified in all their powers
When making love in April showers

Inside you there's a garden
Where precious flowers grow
The fruit of Love abundant thrives
And refreshing rivers flow

So colorful your garden
A Rainbow treat to view
With treasures that reach upward
To catch the morning dew

Patience is a Lily
Compassion is a Rose
Emotion is a Violet rare
Whose beauty brightly glows

I'm in awe of what a sweetness
With which you fill the air
The Birds and bees adore you
The winds play in your hair

And I am the most fortunate
Of all who live and breathe
That I may tend your garden
What a blessing, I believe

And as I behold the glory
Of all that grows in you
The Beauty and the sweetness
That makes my life anew

I give thanks to the Creator
For the work he put in you
A precious gift and treasure
For all the world to view

Breezes blow from nothern skies
Leaves that change before my eyes
Autumn colors on mountain ranges
The signs of seasons and its changes

As summer bids its sweet farewell
And howling winds a tale must tell
We wave good-bye to summer nights
And reminisce its warm delights

But just a short time, we allow
Cause then is then, and now is now
And here we are just you and I
In Love beneath the autumn sky

And though the chill of winter lies
Just days away, we realize
That evermore, despite the weather
It's you and I in love forever

How I long to say I love you
To let the words flow from my lips
As easy as the Mountain streams
Flow from its mighty tips

Constantly I hear these words
They echo in my mind
I long to say I love you
Each day a thousand times

But consider the top of the mountain
At the very, very crest
Wherein there lies a crater
Where only Eagles nest

And deep below the craters mouth
Such mighty power waits
It churns and burns with passions heat
And deeply fascinates

With tantalizing colors
Of black and orange and red
Reflects the colors of the love
That glows inside my head

And though I spout off words of love
So often in a day
It's just to ease the pressure
With these tender words I say

For the day will come when this deep love
Is too great to contain
And all those little spouts of love
Will dissipate like rain

And the mighty crater filled
With all its passion deep inside
Will blow and spew forth all the love
That it has tried to hide

And the word will go from near to far
What God has done in me
To love you by His spirit
Like you never thought could be

Look up into the night sky
Bright stars, oh who could count
Look out across the desert sands
The Infinite amount

Look up into the heavens
Whose bounds are without end
As boundless as the love we share
My lover and my friend

Look down beneath the oceans
Where fathoms pass no light
No place could e'er be deeper
Than the love we share tonight

The spirit that we share, my love
Permeates the outer spaces
And fills the voids of emptiness
And lights the darkened places

How wide must needs the heavens be
A place for to contain it
For nothing in the universe
Could ne'er nor e'er restrain it

Our love is without limits
Our love is without bounds
Our love will soar as Angels do
To endlessness profound

Man cannot live by bread alone
Nor is he an Island, it clearly is shown
But ne'er do I hunger when you are nearby
You fill all my senses, from joy do I cry

For You are a banquet, a sensual delight
The taste of your sweetness makes my soul take flight
I dine on your laughter, your voice fills the air
It penetrates deeply to depths unaware

I feed on your words that fill up my soul
It's your precious love that makes my life whole
Aphrodisia your fragrance, I take with my breath
Your hair, Such a crown for a Queen unto death

I drink in the nectar from your lips so sweet
That drips from your kisses, I'm lost in replete
And feeling the heat of your body near mine
Is just like dessert and feels oh so fine

The wine of your passion, from your cup I take
On the table of life gentle love do we make
For you are the bread of my life, this is true
And life would be famine, were it not for you.

Sitting alone in the dark
A glass of wine touched to my lips
The thoughts of you race through my mind
The love, the life, the pleasure trips

The midnight rides through city streets
Through the park, along the shore
Underneath the moonlit sky
We show each other we adore

We softly kiss, we gently touch
Exploring the senses of pleasure
Inhaling the fragrance of passion pure
Expressing our love, what a treasure

Excuse me if I seem abrupt
I do not mean to interrupt
But I saw you and you looked so fine
And now there's something on my mind

Now looks are just a surface thing
Can't give the joy that love can bring
But what's inside is meant to be
The beauty that I want to see

I'd like to see the love in you
I'd like to know you through and through
I'd like to know your heart and mind
And if your love is warm and kind

I love the lovely way you dress
I long to feel your sweet caress
And press my lips against your face
And feel your radiating grace

To hold you near and feel the heat
And kiss your tender lips so sweet
I'd like to burn in passion's fire
And drown myself in your desire

I'd like to feel the thunder rise
And see the lightning in your eyes
I'd like to hear you cry for more
As crashing waves rush on the shore

I'd like to take you in my world
And let my love for you unfurl
And dress you under stars above
And wrap you in a gown of love

Poets and Prophets, Scholars and Teachers
Professors of Science, Psychics and Preachers
Day in and day out, they search high and low
The mysteries and Questions they all seek to know

The meaning of life, where it came, where it goes
The deepest of secrets, that nobody knows
And I being no different have questions to ask
Some answers come easy, some take you to task

Now the question at hand that sticks in my mind
Is one that an answer's not easy to find
For, of all the things I have wondered and thought
The answer to this one could never be bought

So the Question I ponder and seek to find true
Is... Just which one is better, being alive or loving you?
Then quickly a spirit came near unto me
And opened my eyes so that my mind could see

And showed me the deep things that dwelt in my heart
And made me to know that the two could not part
For our Mighty God has given us life
And a spirit of love, not of conflict and strife

So the only thing left that could make life complete
Is if He gave me you and your love so sweet
Then all of my Questions on life would be done
But one more thing Father, could you please make us one?

There was a place in Europe
A city called Berlin
They built a wall to keep freedom out
And tyranny within

They built a wall in China
Too awesome to behold
That goes for 1500 miles
To protect the land, I'm told

A wall stands in Jerusalem
Twelve gates to represent
Twelve tribes of slaves from Egypt
A Wall of wonderment

And I too want to build a wall
As great as any done
To protect the love that we both share
Until we can be one

This morning I woke up, one more day of living
One more day of loving, one more day of giving
While having my coffee, Enjoying the view
Counting my blessings and thinking of you

I thought of the things that I wanted in life
Especially the things that I want in a wife
Now no one is perfect, that's easy to see
But there are only a few things important to me

I don't want a demon, I don't want a Saint
I don't want to argue what is and what ain't
Now, being realistic, all things you can't be
But here are a few things that you are to me

You're my hope for the future, my bright shining light
My ticket to heaven, my star in the night
My friend and my lover, My Angel on high
My reason for breathing, My answer to "Why?"

You're the start of my morning, the end of my day
My source of direction while I'm on my way
You give me a purpose for staying alive
The reason my heart beats, your love makes me thrive

You're my critical need, you're the reason I love
My gift from the Father in heaven above
So here as I ponder with you on my mind
And all that you are that is loving and kind

And counting the blessings that rain down on me
What more could I want when your love sets me free
So, you see, I'm not picky, my needs are but few
But love, all I'm needin I'm findin in you

The sun does not rise without knowing that it rises on you.
To bring life to the flower that you are.
To open your petals of warmth and affection,
So that you might radiate the love that He has put in you.
To give Freshness to the day, to give color to the eye
To enhance the beauty all around You

I have watched in awe
As the morning light pierces the window
And you begin to unfold and reach for me
As the Rose reaches for the Heavens.

I take treasure in the moments
That I am one with you and with nature
In the same instance, loving a woman
And holding a flower

I am intoxicated by the sweet aroma He has given you.
I am overjoyed as your branches enfold me
And I breathe in your essence.
With passion and purpose, I will love this flower
Until it becomes a seed, and this seed becomes new life
And I will love you again and again... Forever

While on a journey through time and space
The sounds of life my ears embrace
I hear the birds in singing splendor
The sighs of lovers in surrender

The melodies played by the wind
As leafy branches bow and bend
Raindrops on my window pane
Nature's choir in sweet refrain

And then my ears beheld a sound
Like nothing else I'd been around
I pared my senses to find the source
And found it came from you, of course

So soft and sweet, I heard your voice
It made my heart and mind rejoice
For, in your voice true love I hear
And now I know that love is near

For you have sparked such deep desire
Come near my love and feel the fire
And if your heart is hale and fit
I'll spend my whole life loving it

I'll spend my days just loving you
And do for you all I can do
With love, your heart and mind I'll bathe
And all my love for you I'll save

And though my life is filled with sound
And lovely music all around
A perfect life would be my choice
If I could just be near your voice

Today when my eyes met the morn
My heart and mind were forlorn
My countenance had fallen down
My spirit pummeled to the ground

But then my eyes beheld you there
And remembering how much you care
In you my love I put my trust
My heart is yours, that is a must

And so as you so sweetly awaken
My breath is oh so quickly taken
The thought of hearing tones from you
Makes my heart race at speeds untrue

So many times you've made my day
So often chased my blues away
And put that first smile on my face
And filled my heart with shining grace

A word from you can light my soul
And help me gain my self control
My day so gently turned around
A softly lighted way is found

The sun itself when shining bright
Could not withstand your loving light
That shows me there's a brighter way
And starts me with a brighter day

Though I've never seen your face
And I've never heard your voice
Just having got to meet you
Is just cause to rejoice

Cause I've learned so much about you
That I feel we have a bond
I could soar with you forever
To the heavens and beyond

You've touched my heart in many ways
You reached into my soul
You've made my mind to love you
And thoughts of you to hold

Like rains upon a desert
You quench my aching thirst
You wash my heart with tenderness
The dams of love have burst

You overflow the riverbeds
That lie within my mind
You flood the streams of happiness
With loving ways so kind

So now I've seen your heart and mind
I'll tell you what I'll do
Ain't nothing gonna stop me now
From getting close to you

I'm bringing love and tenderness
To you I'll freely give
For you have been my just cause
To want to love and live

If I looked in your face
What would I see
Charm, Grace, Humility?

If I looked in your eyes
What would be there
Flames of fire beyond compare?

If I looked in your heart
What would I find
The fruit of the spirit
To love and be kind

If I promised to love you
And always be true
And give every fiber
Of myself to you

Could I look at you then
And with all of my heart
Love you with passion
Til death do us part?

I know that I want to
I know that I could
To love you forever
I could and I should

As Darkness drifts across the land
And sleeping lovers touch the hand
The crowing cock, the vigilant one
Heralds the wakening of the sun

And through the window, morning's light
Reveals the passing of the night
As gently we begin to stir
A tender sigh exudes from her

Her tender voice drifts in my ear
And reaching for her to come near
Makes all the man within me scream
My God, My God, she's such a dream

And as our bodies draw to meet
Touching lips and touching feet
Sends throes of passion head to toe
Like mighty rivers, juices flow

We climb the mountain, not to stop
To reach the mighty mountain top
The fire grows as we ascend
To each one's needs we do attend

And finally when the sun is high
We reach that mountain in the sky
And give thanks to the Lord above
For sending us Good Morning Love

Candles in wine bottles
Lit the dim room
The sound of sweet music
The scent of perfume

With kisses of Hunger
We draw the deep sigh
With pulsating rhythm
Our hearts start to fly

Sensations electric
Rush swift through our veins
With passion and purpose
We hold to the reins

We give up our minds
We surrender our hearts
With promises precious
We never will part

And with loving and kindness
The Lord up above
Sends Angels of mercy
To watch over our love

At an instant when blessings were being poured out, I saw you.
Nothing more beautiful have my eyes beheld
As if you were a special flower sown only for me
And tended by the Great Spirit of love

I have seen the rising of the Great Northern lights
In all the magnificence of brightness and wonder
Neither Brighter, nor more wonderful than the light in you.
You are the light of my world

I have watched the Honeybee make love to the flowers
Receiving the pollen from one
Leaving new life for regeneration in another
Neither giving nor receiving with more love and grace than you possess
You are the source of life that feeds my soul that it should bear fruit.

I have bathed in the gentle spring rains
That refresh the air leaving a newness to the day and
Magnifying its aromatic beauty. But, never so much
As the refreshing words that come from you
That bathe and soothe my heart and mind
And shower my spirit with peace and serenity

When you look into the heavens
And you see the stars above
And the wonders of creation
Calls to mind a boundless love

Do you ever stop to ponder
Just to reminisce a few
Do you ever stop to think about
Just how much I love you

This love I have is mighty
As the Power of the sun
And I'll shine it down on you my love
To warm you, precious one

No wider could the heavens be
Than this love I have for you
Endless is its vastness
And its course is straight and true

So if you think about me
As you go through your day
Remember this...My love for you
Will never fade away

LIFE

How does it feel when a promise is broken
When words that bring hope are so recklessly spoken
When high flying spirits come crashing to earth
And you look at yourself and you question your worth

Do we just think when a promise is made
And there is no fulfillment, no price must be paid?
Of course there's a cost, there are feelings involved
Emotions within us that must be resolved

A promise so often can lift up one's spirit
Excitement can fill us the moment we hear it
For those who expect us to honor our word
Have pinned so much hope on the promise they heard

But when all that was hopeful turns to despair
Then comes the feeling, you don't really care
So always remember, when a promise is spoken
That a heart may break too when a promise is broken

OH WORLD

Oh World, Oh World, incline your ear
And heed what's in the atmosphere
Raise your heads towards the skies
And see what's right before your eyes

For times have come to test us all
To see if we shall stand or fall
To see if we can long endure
A way of living, so unsure

For as days turn into history
Has love turned into misery?
Oh world, have we forgot our best
And turned our minds to selfishness

Have we pulled in the helping hand
And left the children without a stand
Neglected the aged and the afflicted
Forgot the downtrodden and the addicted

And as we spiral towards destruction
Is there any thought of pain reduction?
You may forget what's going down
But don't forget, it comes around

Oh world please open up your eyes
And come to know and realize
That Brothers and sisters all are we
So World try love and harmony

INSPIRATION

Roses are red, violets are blue
You'll be a winner in all that you do
Just keep your head up with a positive mind
And you will bear fruit, the wonderful kind

Never let anything stand in your way
Just keep moving forward each night and each day
And if you get tired, then sit down to rest
But when resting is over, get back to the test

Keep your eyes on the prize and your focus intact
And you'll make it through, that's a matter of fact
For God is your strength and he may let you fall
But He'll pick you back up and help you stand tall

Mama's at home, alone
Can't do for herself
Sister is carrying the burden
Her life on the shelf
And the call went out
And the men stood up
And the boys did nothing

Pop is in a nursing home
Didn't want to be there
But ne'er a child would visit
Like they just don't even care
And the call went out
And the men stood up
And the boys did nothing

A child is on the street
His life with no direction
The need for one to guide
And foster introspection
And the call went out
And the men stood up
And the boys did nothing

Oh where has flown compassion
Has Love evaporated
Let all the men stand up
When the boys have dissipated
And the call went out
And the men stood up
And the boys took notice

So let them bear the standard
Let the men take hold the reins
And let all the boys take notice
For we're brothers just the same
And the call went out
And the men stood up
And the boys became men

When you're all alone and hurting
And you can't hold back the tears
And the thought of having no one
Magnifies your deepest fears

When you can't think for remembering
All the things you long to share
Cause your heart is filled with vibrant love
And there's no one special there

And inside you know protecting
Is the thing you have to do
Defend your heart at every turn
And keep it safe with you

Don't give it out to anyone
Though that's the main objective
But just who can you give it to
You become much too selective

And you keep a little distance
From all who catch your eye
So that when that final moment comes
No one will see you cry

And back here in your lonely room
The tears stream down your face
And you're reeling from the hurt and pain
That fills this lonely space

But think about your options
While your heart is safe with you
You cry and shiver all night long
And don't know what to do

No sense in being despondent
Why dwell upon the bad
There is treasure rare inside you
That you never knew you had

You were made a Queen by heaven
Only you can take control
Of the dimly burning Beacon
That lights your precious soul

Turn up the light inside you
As you're searching for your pride
The One who made you who you are
Is right there by your side

And if you ask in patience
He'll send you love so true
Til then my heart is with you
And the One WHO IS, is too

There are secrets you may never know
There are things that you may wonder
For life is but a mystery
A spell that we are under

And every day we seek to find
More knowledge of these things
We Educate, we graduate
But still what does it mean

How great it is for me to know
The beauty that's in you
That you have done such great things
You've risen and you flew

You gained knowledge and you stood up
You trudged on and you achieved
You asserted and you shined bright
You excelled and you believed

You came to know a new you
You arrived and you stood out
With the knowledge you've acquired
You're a star, there is no doubt

But the thing that you know least about
And the secret that rings true
Is how deeply way down in my heart
I'm so in love with you

I wake up in the morning
To meet another day
And face the trials and tests of life
As I go on my way

To help the day go smoother
To see my way along
I lift my voice up to the sky
And sing a little song

Amazing what a song can do
To chase the blues away
A lovely tune played in my mind
That brightens up my day

A song that fills my heart with joy
A lilt that lifts my spirit
A melody that won't let go
It soothes my soul to hear it

Though the words are not important
I sing the whole day through
Cause I just want the world to know
The song I sing is you

HOPING

Good Morning my friend, how are you today
Here's hoping that sunshine is coming your way
Here's hoping that showers of blessings will fall
Here's hoping that storm clouds will fade away all

Here's hoping your wishes in life may come true
And all of the love in the world flows to you
Here's hoping that love may make living so sweet
And someone so special makes your life complete

Here's hoping that someone will love you so dear
With muscle and fiber to hold you so near
Here's hoping that strong arms will hold you so tight
And sweet tender kisses will bid you goodnight

Here's hoping that passion will flow like a stream
And someone so loving will fulfill your dream
Here's hoping that all of these things come your way
In portions abundant, forever, I pray

Last night as you lay down to sleep
There were tear drops in your eyes
The pains of life had wrapped you up
And caught you by surprise

This Morning as you awakened
There were storm clouds in your life
There were heartaches that you suffered
And with hurt your mind was rife

But was it ever told to you
That life was just a breeze
That all things would just come to you
And go the way you please?

Did you think it would be easy
A nice stroll through the park
And now your mind is racing
As you sit here in the dark

Tomorrow is your future
And some changes must be made
It's time to focus on the light
And come out of the shade

For another dawn arises
Don't let it bring you grief
The rising of the morning sun
Will bring to you relief

Stand up and face the morning
With the strength that you possess
And the Almighty Creator
Will make it be your best

One Morning as I woke up
Not really knowing how
I pondered life and living
And the Breath that I draw now

I thought about the power
That sustains my beating heart
A power that I could not see
But of which I am a part.

No matter what you call it
What ever name you give
There is an awesome power
That gives us strength to live

So, Give thanks to the power
That made the seeds to grow
That made the gentle rains to fall
And mighty rivers flow

Give thanks to the power
That made the mighty sun
That lights the day and lights the way
Until our lives are done

Give thanks to the power
For all you have received
For peace and comfort in the night
At times when you were grieved

Give thanks to the power
That brought you through the storm
That wiped the tear drops from your eyes
And kept you safe and warm

Give thanks to the power
That comes from up above
For all the good that comes to us
Comes by the power of love

So, Give thanks to the power
In a very special way
For Everyday we open our eyes
It is Thanksgiving day